THE WEALTH MOTO

PROPERTY

Money Matters

by Gill Fielding

FOREWORD

The Wealth Company's philosophy is to facilitate financial freedom for people by showing them that the pathway to wealth is a three lane wealth motorway.

This book is about the property lane of the motorway and provides some of the information necessary for people to decide what type of property investment suits them best.

It is important to remember that this book is not prescriptive nor should it be construed as specific advice for you – it is information from which you make your own choices – and you should always speak to a professional adviser if you want assistance with that choice.

I offer you my support and encouragement along your journey – and please contact us at www.wealthcompany.com if you want or need any further guidance or assistance.

Gill Fielding

Gill Fielding
Founder

CONTENTS

INTRODUCTION

The money matters when you are investing in property – or does it? There are so many possibilities available to us nowadays that what used to be the biggest stumbling block - the money - now has diminishing importance. We read constantly of 'no money down deals', seller finance deals and lease options purchase and perhaps the money is not now the most important thing. Perhaps the most important thing nowadays is the awareness of these type of investment deals and the ability to make informed and positive choices: choices that suit you and your circumstances and your investment strategy.

So this book is about all the financial aspects of investing in property: the old and the new, the established and the wacky, and hopefully there will be some piece of information in here that helps you along your own personal path to financial freedom.

What this book isn't of course, is personal advice, and in all cases I suggest you read the information, work out what appeals to you and why, and then take that information to a financial adviser. That way you will be informed enough to make the right choice when the adviser offers that choice.

I hope that something here lights the spark of financial possibility for you – so read, do your research and have fun!

information that helps you along your own personal path to financial freedom

INTRODUCTION - THE BASICS

The subject of property finance is a big and complex area and scary for most people. Undaunted however we will now stroll through the main topics in this area and hopefully demystify the subject matter. At the end of the day most financial products, when unravelled, are quite simple, but appear confusing purely because they are unfamiliar, defined in confusing jargon and jumbled together to look like scrambled egg!

Where does the money come from?

The money to buy property comes from anywhere and everywhere. Although the main finance will probably come from a financial services company in some way – probably in the shape of a mortgage, you may still need to find a deposit. How can you find this deposit; your seed capital to start your investment portfolio?

The seed capital or deposit

You may be able to get your first deposit from an investment group, where you club together to form a syndicate with your friends, family or fellow investors. Ideally, you join with people with similar investment strategies and all chip in a certain amount. In some cases people bring resources and skills to the syndicate other than money and most property investor bulletin boards on the internet have syndicate requests. There are now many well known and substantial property syndicates, such as Property in Britain Ltd, which all started in this way

Or,

- you might actually have, or save up the deposit money yourself

- you might borrow from your friends, family or colleagues

- you might get loans, overdrafts or credit of some kind

- you might release funds from a pension (which can be difficult and generally only works if you are over 50)

- you might release equity from your own home, and of course………

- you might actually obtain a full mortgage or finance from an external fund provider.

All these methods of raising finance for property investment are fine, and all you need to do is to find the right source of finance for you.

Certainly, finding the seed capital for the very first purchase is always the most difficult, as with any subsequent investment you have some huge benefits:

1   You've done it before, so you feel more confident, which helps your investment decisions.

2   You've done it before and fund providers like you more.

3   You already have an asset (the first purchase) which you can use (in full or in part) as collateral or security for the next loan.

4   You've done it before so you feel more comfortable and relaxed and less scared about the whole process.

Oh, and did I mention:

5   You've done it before!

> **TOP TIP**
>
> It is always easier to get funding on something you already own than something you don't! So you'll find it much easier to mortgage or re-mortgage a property once you have it in your portfolio

OTHER PEOPLE'S MONEY: LEVERAGE OR GEARING

Many of you will have read or heard the adage that it is better to use other people's money when investing, but why? It is because using other people's money gives us the benefits of gearing, and we have the benefit of the gain on the whole of the investment when we have only put in a little. It is certainly true that the less we put into a deal the higher the return on our money.

Gearing and use of other people's money (and we can include the money that 'belongs' to banks and building societies), gives us a huge potential that generally our own money can not.

Let us see how gearing works with an example.

If we assume that:

- we have £100,000 of our own money to invest

- we want to buy property with that amount

- house prices are rising at 10% per year, and

- we have access to other people's money through mortgages.

Scenario 1: we just use our own money

If we invest our £100,000 in one property for one year, at the end of that year our property is worth (at 10% growth) £110,000. We have made a £10,000 gain on our property. Not bad for a one year investment.

Scenario 2: we use our own money ADDED to other people's money

If we invest the £100,000 as a deposit and obtain a mortgage we could buy a property worth £1,000,000 – assuming that we get a 90% mortgage. The same year passes, the same rate of growth at 10% is made, but at the end of the year in this version of events, our property is worth £1,100,000. In this instance an increase of £100,000 not £10,000.

Ask yourself: would you rather make a capital gain of £10,000 or £100,000 in one year using exactly the same starting capital?

By using mortgages and other people's money you can leverage or gear up the value of your investments to make a huge difference over as little as one year.

Even more powerful is the thought that if we continued this simple example over 25 years, and property prices continued to rise at 10%, the difference between the value of the two properties at the end of 25 years would be an amazing:

£9,751,235!

So if you refuse to use other people's money and mortgages you are denying yourself one opportunity of being a multi millionaire in your lifetime – do you really want to do that!

Before we start, it is worth thinking about mortgages from the finance providers' or lenders' perspective. All the financial providers at some time have money to lend: in fact there is more money out there waiting to find borrowers than there is demand from us to borrow that money.

Each financial service provider is in business to make money and constantly has business targets to meet, they actually need to be providing mortgages or they go bust. So put yourself in their place and you can see that they need to be providing mortgages for you in order to make money and stay in business. This acts as a massive motivation for them to loan you money – just imagine that – they really, really want to be able to provide you with investment money, all you have to do is ask for it – and ask for it in the right way.

On top of that there are many thousands of different financial services products out there waiting for you. There are mortgages for the self-employed, for the unemployed and for the fully employed. There are mortgages for old people, young people, groups of people, pairs and individuals. There WILL be a financial product out there that suits your particular situation and circumstances – you may have to search through perhaps 7,000 sources to find it, but it WILL be there!

As a guide just go into www.google.co.uk and type in a particular funding type, say "bad credit mortgages", and see what pops up! I am constantly amazed by the variety and number of different funding options there are. I am sure that there will be some provider who specialises in funding for every type of person and every type of strategy.

Remember: there is more money out there waiting to be borrowed than there is demand for that money: so get some today.

So what are the basic mortgage types?

There are two basic groups of mortgages, those that include an element of capital in each repayment (which is normally monthly) and those that don't.

Repayment mortgage

This is the 'old fashioned' mortgage that most of us know and love. Many of us have had a repayment mortgage in the past. The repayment mortgage is normally over a 25 year term (but can be any period in length), in which each monthly payment made includes an interest element and a capital element. The interest is charged on the principal (or capital) amount outstanding and the capital is repaid over the period of the mortgage. Although the monthly payment amounts don't vary significantly over the term, at the beginning of these mortgages the monthly repayment is almost entirely interest and by the end of the term the repayment is almost entirely capital. However, it is worth noting that over the 25 years of these mortgages the total repayments typically amount to 2 or 3 times the original capital loan amount, so the total repayments over 25 years on a £100,000 loan would certainly be in excess of £250,000.

Interest only mortgage

An interest only mortgage does exactly what it says on the tin! It is where your monthly repayment covers only the interest on the principal borrowed over the course of the mortgage term. In some cases there is separate provision made to accumulate an amount equal to the capital principle borrowed, such that when the term of the mortgage ends, there is a lump sum somewhere available to pay off the original loan. Endowments are one form of this; ISA (or PEP) mortgages are another and pension mortgages are a third. In all these cases some extra money per month goes into some other savings vehicle that is expected to generate a sufficient return to produce a sizeable lump sum after time.

However, these additional capital producing products are not compulsory when taking out an interest only mortgage. But for your own sanity I suggest that you consider how you intend to repay the capital at the end of the mortgage period. For most professional property investors their options are that:

- they do not intend to hold the property for the full length of the mortgage anyway and will repay the principal from any sales proceeds, or

- they intend to have enough properties in their portfolio such that paying off a mortgage here or there is possible from either the income they are generating or from capital gain over the whole or part of, their portfolio, and finally,

- if the value of property continues to increase, then mortgages can easily be repaid with some of the profits from the investment (perhaps from re-mortgaging).

Remember that on average each house is sold every 7 years.

MORTGAGES - WHAT DO I NEED TO ASK?

1 How much can I borrow?

The answer is – it depends!

If you are applying for a normal domestic residential mortgage then the amount you can borrow will almost certainly be based on your income together with the income of your partner.

However, when purchasing an investment property as a business transaction, it is much more likely that the amount you can borrow will be determined by the property (or the investment) itself. Firstly, the amount that you can borrow is usually determined by the value of the property in question. It is fairly standard that we can borrow 80% LTV (Loan To Value – which simply means the loan or mortgage is, in this case, 80% of the property value), and it is relatively common to borrow 90% or perhaps more.

It is also possible to obtain a loan or a mortgage for 100% of the property value and in some extreme circumstances you can get mortgages of up to 135% of the property value. These higher percentages however, will normally only be available on domestic residential mortgages.
The web site:
www.mortgagesonline.co.uk has a section that lists the top 10 mortgages of varying criteria – so have a look.

2 Yes, but how much can I borrow?

Assuming that the loan does not exceed the lenders LTV criteria, the amount you can borrow depends very much on your own personal circumstances and the type of mortgage you are aiming to get.

There are four basic approaches to qualifying for mortgages:

- If you have a full time job, and evidence (such as payslips) of regular and recurring income

- If you have your own business and you have accounts for a certain number of years (usually between 3 and 5 years)

- If you are self employed and you estimate your own income: this is called 'self certification'

- If you have no earned income at all or you don't want to declare any, you may still get certain mortgages, such as buy-to-let mortgages based on some other income, such as the rental income from the property being purchased, or on other properties in your portfolio.

Now, as a general rule, the more 'secure' your income, the more choices of mortgage you will have and the lower the interest rate you will pay. However, this is not always the case and certain mortgage providers are much happier about, say, self certification than others, and their interest rates will probably be similar to standard rates. Other providers get nervous when they see 'self certification' on the application form and will immediately increase the interest rate.

So the mortgage you get and the interest you pay depends on you, your income sources, the particular finance provider and the investment strategy you are implementing. You must search to get the right financial product for your particular circumstances.

3 What is the standard term or life of a mortgage?

In the UK we are used to mortgage terms traditionally of 25 years, or sometimes a bit longer. However, most finance providers will happily provide you with a mortgage for 5 years, 13 years, 19 years, 27 years or whatever you need to suit your circumstances. Mortgage terms as a general rule are getting longer, and we now see 35-year mortgages. In some parts of the world mortgage terms are much longer, and in Japan the mortgage can run for more than a lifetime and the loan as well as the property is bequeathed to the children!

4 How do the interest rates vary?

Most mortgage interest rates in the UK are connected in some way to the Bank of England base rate. Now this rate is often called many other things, but fundamentally it is the headline rate that you see announced on the news and in the newspapers. Most mortgages are connected to this base rate, as follows:

- **A tracker mortgage** is one that tracks the base rate exactly. So you may be paying a small amount, say 0.5%, above base and when the base rate rises, so does your mortgage interest and when the base rate is reduced, so are your payments.

  Beware here though that mortgage providers can sometimes be slow in reflecting reductions in Bank of England base rate and can be quick to raise them as soon as there is a sniff of a Base rate increase. So the lenders will play the game their way and there's nothing you can do about it – but just be aware.

- **A standard variable rate mortgage** is similar to a tracker in that it moves in line with the base rate but sometimes with a time delay and not always by the same amount as movements in the base rate. A standard variable rate mortgage will normally be between 0.25 and 1% above base.

- **A capped mortgage** is where the interest rate is capped at a certain maximum level by the lender. Where the interest rate is capped upwards and downwards, it is called a 'collared' mortgage.

- **A discounted mortgage** is when you get finance at a discount to the base rate or the banks variable rate. This discounted interest rate normally applies for a given period and then reverts to a standard or higher rate. These mortgages are designed to help you get started as the initial payments are held low.

- **A fixed rate mortgage** enables you to budget accurately and with certainty as the interest rate is fixed for some of the mortgage term. These mortgages are very popular with first time buyers as they fix rates for the first few years after which the mortgage normally reverts to a standard variable rate. In this case, you win if the rates go up as your rate is fixed at a lower percentage, but you lose if rates go down. The provider would normally fix the interest rate for 1, 2 or 5 years.

- **A commercial mortgage** is one that is generally provided only for commercial properties. It will probably be at a slightly higher interest rate and is generally for larger sums of money than a domestic mortgage. Sometimes people refer to commercial mortgages when they mean funds provided for a business rather than for an individual.

- **A flexible mortgage** is a loan where the interest is charged daily rather than monthly, quarterly or annually which generally means that you pay less interest! The interest rate is generally a standard variable rate. The mortgage is also flexible in that you can pay flexible amounts, miss occasional payments and overpay when you are able. Some variants allow you to draw down more money within given limits without having to re-mortgage. So it does provide you with a lot more flexibility in your mortgage payments and this works particularly well if your income is erratic.

The money to be saved with flexible mortgages can be staggering, as every penny counts to reduce the interest charge. Due to compounding, overpayments save huge amounts over time, and also reduce the term of the mortgage substantially.

5 What is an offset mortgage?

An offset or current account mortgage is a flexible mortgage where all your financial balances with one provider are added together each day to create a net balance due to the bank. You are then charged interest on this lower balance. So if you have £50,000 on a mortgage and £5,000 on deposit as savings with your financial provider, you will only pay interest on the net of £45,000. This is a huge bonus and is particularly advantageous for people who have large amounts of cash washing around their current accounts during the month. It also has a great tax benefit in that you are not taxed on deposit interest earned, because clearly you don't receive any as the deposit is used to offset against your mortgage loan. This is a big advantage particularly with higher rate tax payers.

6 What's an investment mortgage?

An investment mortgage is one where the funds are provided for an investment business to purchase, in this case, properties. The mortgages are normally based on the financial position of the business itself. So the fund provider will check the viability of the business by checking:

• that the property values are appropriate for the funding, and

• that the business has enough income to service the mortgage repayments. They do this normally by specifying that the rentals generated are perhaps 125% or 130% of the proposed mortgage repayments.

So, if you hear fund providers asking for a 130% ratio of rent to mortgage you know they are looking for the rent to cover the mortgage payments by 130%. If the mortgage payments are £1,000 per month, the rent needs to be at least £1,300 in this case. These ratios are normally between 125% - 135%.

The standard investment mortgage that we have in the UK now is the Buy-To-Let mortgage which enables you to buy property for investment purposes. It also comes in a variety of options, and you can get discounted, capped, fixed and variable buy-to-let mortgages just as listed above. The interest rates may be slightly higher than those for normal residential mortgages and it is currently more difficult to obtain a 100% buy-to-let mortgage.

When buy-to-let mortgages were first introduced, most providers would only lend 70% of loan to value. This percentage has gradually increased over time and now 85% mortgages are common and 90% mortgages are sometimes available.

Similarly interest rates on buy-to-let mortgages used to be considerably higher than the interest rates on residential mortgages but as competition in the mortgage market has increased this difference in interest rates has nearly disappeared.

Buy-to-let mortgages also vary considerably in length and can start from as short as 5 years, and stretch up to 50 years.

7   What special offers can I get?

Depending on the state of their business, financial providers will often offer substantial perks and benefits for dealing with them. They are obviously trying to get your business and are trying to make it as easy as possible for you to transact with them. The offers that are generally available include:

- Cash back at completion. This is where the mortgage provider will offer you an amount as cash as a 'refund' or cash back when you complete on your purchase. This can vary from a fixed amount, say £200, to a percentage of the loan, say, 5% of the loan amount. These offers can be fairly tempting as you receive money when you need it most – at the beginning – but generally with these offers there will be an early redemption penalty clause (see below) attached and perhaps a higher interest rate.

- Some lenders will offer 'free' conveyancing or a contribution towards your legal costs. There may occasionally be strings attached to this and they may ask that you use their nominated or in house lawyer rather than your own.

- When a financial provider agrees to lend money to you they always have their own valuation report. In most cases, you, the borrower pay for this report. However, one benefit occasionally offered is to waive this valuation fee.

- Free or cheap insurances are also sometimes offered, and you may find that this insurance is actually from another arm of the mortgage provider's business – but hey, if it's free then take it! If it is only free for a limited period – then dump the insurance provider at the end of the free period, unless the insurance product is the best you can get.

- Often with new build houses, you will be offered a certain amount of free furniture, fittings, carpets, bathrooms and kitchen equipment by the builder.

TOP TIP

In all cases when you are buying a property, whether as an investor or as a homeowner, then always ask for ALL the above. You may get some or may you may not, but if you don't ask, you don't get!

One thing to be wary of with all these deals is to check that the developer or seller doesn't just add the cost of these benefits to the principal of the loan!

8   What nasty news should I watch out for?

a)   The early redemption charge or the redemption penalty.

In most cases where a discounted or capped interest rate is offered, you will find that there is an early redemption charge or redemption penalty also attached to the loan. This means, for instance, that there may be a penalty for redeeming the mortgage early that can be significant: perhaps 6 months interest or refund of the total benefit or discount received. Clearly redemption penalties are aimed to lock in the customer for as long as possible. A redemption 'overhang' is where the redemption penalty clause is for a longer period than the original benefit. So where a redemption penalty period is in force for, say 4 years, when the discounted rate applied for only 2.

b)   Lenders valuation fees.

As explained above, the lender will always insist on getting their own valuation for any property that they lend on. It is curious however, that they need this valuation for their own purposes, but we, the borrower generally have to pay for it. Also if the deal falls through this fee is not refunded.

Note, that even though you have paid for the lenders valuation, you will normally not be allowed to see it.

> **TOP TIP**
>
> Finance providers have their own panel of approved valuers, and so you may be able to save some money by using a valuer for your own valuation or survey purposes, who is on the lenders panel. The valuer can then give some discount for valuing the same property for two people.

c)   Insurances.

Occasionally lenders will try to guide you towards using their own insurance company for instance for the buildings insurance, or accident, sickness and unemployment insurances. Please be aware that lenders cannot make it a condition of any loan that you take their particular insurance or other service and to do so is a breach of the relevant legislation.

However, they can make the loan conditional upon you taking out some appropriate buildings insurance.

d)   Mortgage indemnity charge, or mortgage indemnity guarantee.

Also known as the high percentage fee. Some lenders insist on you paying this fee or charge if they feel that the amount borrowed is too close to the actual value of the property. So if for example, you get a 95% mortgage, the lender may ask for you to pay for this guarantee such that if the property value falls, then the lenders money is protected by the guarantee.

NB. If this guarantee is called upon, the lender gets the money and not you!

e)   Booking fees or arrangement fees.

This is normally paid to the lender and is attached to the loan application form. It may be a fixed amount or a percentage of the loan amount requested. The booking fee will not be refundable if the loan is not granted.

Arrangement fees tend to be the fee charged by the lender at the other end, i.e. when the loan is granted to you. These fees are more commonly seen on fixed or capped rate mortgages.

f)   Other fees and charges

Yes, there are plenty! And they will vary from lender to lender and will be called different things. So please be aware of them, ask your questions about fees very clearly and make sure that you get the full picture before you sign anything!

9 What can I use as security for a mortgage?

In short everything and anything that the lender will agree to! You can use any, some or all of the following:

- the property you are buying

- your existing home (perhaps as a second mortgage)

- your existing property portfolio – if you already have one

- other assets or businesses that the lender will accept as security

- other income streams, in the form of a guarantee.

Note: that the asset you use as collateral or security for the loan need not even be in this country – so just ask the lender if that possibility exists for you.

10 Can I have more than one mortgage per property?

Absolutely! Yes you can. You can have several mortgages on one property. They do not need to be with the same lender, as long as the terms and conditions of each loan allow for multiple mortgages. You will discover that the first or original lender will have 'first charge' over the property and other subsequent mortgages will have second charges.

You can see all the charges that are attached to your property by looking at the Land Registry on: www.landreg.gov.uk

You can even have several mortgages on each property and you would then have several charges over the property registered. So if you have a mortgage with a bank plus a loan from your auntie to pay for the deposit, they would both be valid charges on the register. The only warning here is that you need to check with each individual lender if they agree to this – because some don't.

It is important to understand the priority of charges over a property and they indicate the order in which monies are distributed in the case of default on the mortgage where the property is repossessed. So the first charge owner gets first grab at any money, then the second charge holder and so on down the chain – and then you get what's left over, if any!

TOP TIP

When you clear or pay off a mortgage always check with the lender that they have removed the charge at the Land Registry, because sometimes they forget to do this.

MORTGAGES - WHAT DO I NEED TO ASK?

11 Are you sure that I will be able to get a mortgage?

The answer to this must be that yes you will, as long as you are prepared to pay the price!

There are mortgages for people with bad credit and with CCJ's (County Court Judgments) against them.

There are mortgages for people with great credit.

There are mortgages for people who want to buy a run down property and renovate it: www.renovationmortgages.co.uk

There are mortgages for first time buyers, for those re-mortgaging or taking out second or third or fourth mortgages.

There are mortgages for ecologically friendly projects and accelerated mortgages where you get stage payments as you develop or renovate the property.

There are mortgages for listed buildings, new buildings, incomplete buildings and mortgages for converting windmills – if you want one!

The next time you are shopping buy a copy of a magazine like What Mortgage, which lists different mortgage types and calculation methods and can be an appropriate place to start looking for finance.

Also, try searching around these web sites for your particular need:

www.mortgage.loanspage.co.uk www.ukloanshop.co.uk
www.moneyquest.co.uk
www.adversecreditmortgagesontheweb.co.uk
www.mortgagehunters.net
www.moneysupermarket.com/mortgages
www.Quote4mortgages.co.uk
www.uk250.co.uk/Finance

There will certainly be one of the several thousand financial products out there that will suit your specific purpose and fortunately you will NOT be unique and somebody somewhere will have been in your particular circumstances before.

As a regular exercise, go to www.google.co.uk (or any search engine on the internet) and enter a search for a specific mortgage type – and as well as the list above, google will come up a huge variety of web sites for you to check. There are new sites appearing every week so watch out for new developments.

12 Can I get a mortgage if I want to buy a property at auction?

Yes you can, and you will find specialist mortgage brokers who deal almost exclusively with the auction market. To find one look for their adverts in Auction Catalogues, or in auction magazines. To research the auctions possibilities put 'property auctions' into www.google.co.uk and see what pops up – there will be many sites, one of which is www.ukpad.co.uk

At auctions you will generally be required to place a 10% deposit when your bid is accepted, and then provide the remainder of the money within 28 days.

13 How many mortgages can I have?

There is no legal limit to the number of mortgages you can have, so it's a case of finding as many as you want. There are some mortgage providers who will set a limit on the number of mortgages with them, at, say, 5 or 10 mortgages, but when you have reached the limit on one, then go to another lender.

You will soon find that some lenders are more accommodating to this than others, and you may find that you want to spread your net quite widely to give yourself as much access to as many lenders as possible.

Also be aware that if you think you may want multiple mortgages then a line of credit or a block of mortgages may be a better deal for you. So in this case you arrange with a mortgage lender that you get 'pre approved' for a block of, say 10 mortgages, or for a block amount, say £250,000, to be used and drawn down as and when you find the right properties. The lender will still want to conduct their survey on each property as it comes up, but you will not have to go through the application procedure each time.

This block approach also might show a cleaner position on your personal credit file, as it shows only one transaction rather than several.

14 What is an arrangement or mortgage in principle?

These are sometimes also called guaranteed mortgages, because they are pre approved. In this instance you apply for a mortgage for a property you haven't yet identified and the mortgage company then complete all their checks on you and grant you a mortgage in principle. So they agree to provide you with a certain amount of money based on your circumstances and then all you have to do is find the right property and you are ready to buy. They will issue you with a mortgage certificate that will prove that you are as good as a cash buyer. This gives you the advantage of being able to purchase quickly. Remember that the lender will still want to conduct the normal survey on the property once you have found it.

15 Shall I use a mortgage broker?

A mortgage broker will be able to search through a whole long list of potential mortgage providers and find the best one for you. They will generally have search software that will search potential sources according to your personal circumstances. So say for instance, you want a mortgage with no early redemption penalties, and with a discounted rate. The mortgage broker will be able to find the providers that will loan you money on those terms.

So a mortgage broker may be able to save you some leg work and time.

But don't forget that mortgage brokers have to eat too and they will be paid in some way for their services. They normally receive payment either as a fee (from you) or as commission from the lender. Both ways have their advantages; the commission route seems attractive because you do not have to pay anything directly, but perhaps the fee route gives you greater comfort that you are getting the best deal for you rather than the best commission deal for the broker.

Occasionally the broker will get commission and a fee – but they have to disclose any earnings to you when you deal with them.

Discuss the basis of the payment with the broker before you commit to using them.

As one final point here you should be aware that there are some finance providers that will not deal with you directly even if you beg them. This is to do with the Financial Services Act and the giving of advice, and so in some cases you will have to find a broker to act for you if you want a specific mortgage from a specific lender.

Always make sure that the mortgage broker you are talking to is actually a broker for many different companies and products. This is different to an agent, who will probably only act for, and sell you, one particular lender's products.

TOP TIP

Ask the broker about commission splitting whereby they share the commission from the mortgage company with you.

16 Who can I go to if I have a problem?

There are a variety of regulatory bodies and watchdogs in this area. Most loans are covered by the Mortgage Code but smaller loans (i.e. below £25,000 are covered by the Consumer Credit Act, so you may need different help depending on the size of the loan involved.

Start to look for help at: www.cml.org.uk (council of mortgage lenders) at www.mortgagecode.co.uk

NB Regulations are changing all the time so please ask your broker or support team about new legislation that affects you. You may also be able to keep up with changes by reading property investing periodicals (like Property Auction News) and by visiting property investor chat rooms and information web sites – find them from www.google.co.uk

17 What special conditions might be applied to mortgages?

There are many! And again depend on the attitude taken by your mortgage provider. Some that might apply include restrictions or refusal of loans on properties that:

- are not brick or stone
- do not have a slate, tile or concrete roof
- do not have basic sanitary ware
- are built from a 'kit'
- are in high rise blocks over a certain number of floors
- are ex local authority properties
- are in areas with a predominance of local authority housing
- have too many occupants
- have sitting tenants

and so on. Once again, your best course of action is to ask and keep asking until you find a provider that likes your wood built, kit house on a council estate!

18 What about leaseholds?

As a general rule there is no difference between mortgages for leaseholds and mortgages for freeholds. However, be aware that you need to make sure that there are enough years left in the lease to make the proposition viable. As a rough rule of thumb most providers will ask for leaseholds to be as long as the life of two mortgages. Some lenders interpret this to be 50 years (i.e. twice times 25 years) and some say 60 or even 70 years. To be safe expect leaseholds to have at least 70 years to run before you consider them.

> **TOP TIP**
>
> If you like the look of a leasehold property but the lease isn't long enough, then investigate the possibility of applying to buy the freehold or share of the freehold. Or ask if you can pay for an extension of the lease.

19 Where else can I get a mortgage?

As well as all the usual (probably 3,000 in number) financial institutions there are a variety of sources for mortgages. Consider:

- your local authority
- your employer
- the builder (especially if you are doing an exchange deal)
- finance houses
- credit companies
- insurance companies
- the seller (see later for details).

MORTGAGES - WHAT DO I NEED TO ASK?

20 So which is the best mortgage to have?

The answer is that IT DEPENDS! Hopefully this section will have given you enough information and resources, to start to answer this question yourself as you will clearly see that this is a 'horses for courses' type question and you need to find the mortgage that best suits your circumstances, your strategy and your potential investment.

There is no right or wrong answer to this question but consider the following short guide:

Interest Only Funding

On the one hand....

- monthly payments are lower than for repayment mortgages
- the entire payments are eligible for tax relief (if property is rented out), and makes for a simpler tax return!
- you can use the cash 'saved' for other investments
- interest only mortgages give you a bigger return on your money invested in the property.

But

- you never reduce the loan over the term
- you may have to sell the property at the end to repay the mortgage.

Repayment Mortgage

On the one hand....

- the amount you owe reduces over time
- if you keep up the repayments the property is yours 'free and clear' at the end.

But

- monthly repayments are higher than for interest only funding
- you pay off very little capital in the early years.

Standard Variable Rate

On the one hand....

- easy to understand, and they are familiar to most of us
- linked to the Bank of England Rate, which is well known
- generally carries few or no penalties.

But

- does not take advantage of special rates
- payments fluctuate with interest rates, which means that your overall financial return is less certain.

Discounted Mortgages

On the one hand....

- you get the best deal available at the moment
- monthly payments are as low as possible
- outgoings are lower, particularly in the earlier years.

But

- loss of flexibility as you may be tied in to the specific lender or the specific product for long periods
- early redemption penalties may be significant and severe.

Fixed rates

On the one hand....

- your repayments are fixed for the period stipulated
- certainty and accuracy with budgeting monthly cash flows into the future
- interest rate stays the same for the whole of the agreed period
- you will be better off when interest rates are rising.

But

- loss of flexibility as you may be tied in for long periods
- early redemption penalties may be harsh
- you may lose out if interest rates are falling.

Capped rates

On the one hand....

- security in the knowledge that rises in the interest rate are limited
- will also be able to receive the benefits of interest rate falls (unless it is also a collared mortgage).

But

- loss of flexibility as you may be tied in for long periods
- early redemption penalties may be harsh.

Offset mortgages

On the one hand....

- simple to control your finances if they are all in one place
- every penny that you have goes to reducing your interest payments
- no tax payable on deposit interest earned (savings here can be significant for higher rate tax payers)
- flexibility.

But

- you may pay a slightly higher interest rate.

Flexible mortgages

On the one hand...

- Of course, FLEXIBILITY!
- interest is calculated daily and consequently is lowest
- very easy to get the benefits of overpayments (and the compounding of overpayments)
- easy to draw down extra money, or have payment holidays once your account is in credit, or to pay variable sums
- you may get a cheque book facility with this, which you can use to pay large bills – or to make more investments! when your account is in credit.

But

- discount rates are unusual with flexible accounts
- you need to be disciplined to ensure that you don't fall behind with payments: it is too easy to spend everything!

21 Why does it have to be so complicated?

The answer of course is that it doesn't need to be complicated at all. Partly some finance providers delight in confusing you – so if that happens to you ditch that finance provider - and partly our own fear puts up a 'comprehension barrier' to stop us understanding it.

We all know that if we believe we can't understand something then we never will. So to help yourself, chop all the information down into little bits and tackle a piece per day until you get comfortable. Build up your finance muscles just like you would your abs or pecs. Gradually you will find that the data and information can be broken down and understood easily.

22 So, what are the important things to remember?

It is easy to be confused with the different mortgages on offer and with the amazingly varied terms and conditions. However, all financial products need to be fully explained and understood, so persevere with your financial adviser or mortgage lender until you are confident of what you are getting.

I always believe that if the broker can't explain the mortgage in terms I understand then either the broker doesn't know or s/he is a bad broker. It is too easy to hide ignorance in verbose and technical language that is designed to confuse. Don't accept that!

MORTGAGES: THE CRUNCH POINTS!

Overall then, with mortgages think about asking the following questions:

1   What type of funding is most appropriate or relevant for this particular investment strategy?

2   How long is the mortgage term?

3   How is the interest calculated and what type of interest rate is it: standard, discounted, capped or whatever?

4   What are the charges? get them listed clearly, and then ask again....

5   Are you sure that's **all** the charges?

6   Are there any special terms and conditions attached to this mortgage?

7   Are there any penalties at any stage?

8   How long do you normally take to complete the arrangement of finance?

9   What are the benefits attached to this mortgage?

10 Do you have any special deals or benefits for good customers, repeat customers or long serving customers – if so, ask to have them!

WHAT IF I NEED MONEY FOR REFURBISHMENT?

Firstly remember that many mortgage providers have renovation or refurbishment style mortgages so just ask them. If your normal provider doesn't have this product in their range then look on the internet or in a mortgage magazine (available in most supermarkets and major high street newsagents) for one that does.

After that unfortunately, for most home improvements or refurbishment schemes you will probably have to find the money yourself, but there are some places to look to obtain some grants or funding.

1 **Buy and Refurbish To Let (BARTL) mortgages.**

You can actually get a specific mortgage that just caters for this type of development. Ask your financial provider if they have these, or one company that does is Paragon at: www.paragon-mortgages.co.uk.

2 **Housing Renovation Grants.**

These are available to owners and landlords and the aim is to encourage housing provision, so the local authority will provide grants to help with certain types of refurbishment, as long as the property is then available for lettings for a certain time, say 5 years after the receipt of the grant. Contact your local housing office for details.

3 **Grants for multiple occupancy housing.**

There are two possibilities here: an HMO (House of Multiple Occupancy) grant which is available to landlords only to make houses fit for multiple occupancy: and, a Common Parts Grant available for refurbishment of the communal areas of HMOs.

In all these cases, apply to your local authority for information, or contact the Department for Transport, Local Government and the Regions on 0870 122 6236, or e-mail DLTR@twoten.press.net for an information pack.

4 **VAT concessions.**

There are some VAT concessions, which basically reduce the VAT applicable to certain refurbishments from 17.5% to 5% on the costs of refurbishment if the property has been empty for at least three years; or for conversion of properties into residential units, or an HMO.

Contact the VAT Advice Service for details, on 0845 010 9000.

5 There are other less specific grants available, such as the Heritage Economic Regeneration Scheme (HERS): contact English Heritage on 0870 333 1181 or www.english-heritage.org.uk.

6 Finally, the Community Investment Fund supports small local community projects between £10,000 and £100,000. Contact them on 0207 881 1600 or www.englishpartnerships.org.uk

In the last couple of years there have been many 'new' ideas come into the UK, mainly from America, about how to finance properties creatively or with no money down. Although the Americans have been good at promoting these methods of financing, they have in the main, been used in the UK for many a long year – we just don't seem to have the same knack for publicising our creativity!

So, this section will go through many of the 'new' financing ideas and will explain the mechanics of how they work. It will then be up to you as to how you incorporate them into your own property investment strategy.

Please note that this section is not a recommendation or condemnation of any of the topics or methods described, but is purely an explanation of how the processes work.

1 Seller financing

Much is now written about seller financing and many people appear to make this issue complicated, but in its simplest form, seller financing is purely when the seller provides some of the money for you to buy their property.

The reason many people have difficulties with explaining or understanding this is that they try to understand why on earth anybody would do this. FORGET IT! You will never know why people act as they do, so just go with it and accept that in some cases sellers are willing, and maybe even keen, to put up some money for you.

So how does it work?

Level one

In order to make this simple, let's say that you want to buy a property for £100,000 and you have no money of your own at all. You have arranged a 90% mortgage and you are £10,000 short. What do you do? You may get a personal loan, or get an overdraft from your bank, or you may just borrow the money from your friends or family. We can all see how we could borrow the £10,000 from our best friend or our Dad – well with seller financing in its simplest form, you just go back to the seller and ask to borrow the £10,000 from them. Easy.

In this case, the seller would lend you the £10,000 and you would repay them over an agreed time, at an agreed rate, and an agreed amount per month (or quarter, or week or whatever). You would repay the seller in exactly the same way you would repay your friend or your Dad or your personal loan or the overdraft. You get the property and the seller gets two things. Firstly, they get a motivated buyer for their property and secondly, they probably get a better rate of interest from you, the purchaser, on the £10,000 than they would if they had left their money in the bank. In fact some sellers actively seek these kinds of deal because it is their way of making a turn, or income, on their money.

Let's take it one more step further. If you are a seller with a very good credit rating and you can borrow money easily at say, 5%, it may be a very good idea to borrow money cheaply in order to loan money to other people at higher rates. As security the seller normally gets either a second mortgage or second charge over the property or a loan contract but please check with your primary lender that they are happy with these second charges.

Level Two

Now imagine the same scenario as above, but in this case the seller provides ALL the financing. So you buy a property worth £100,000 but instead of getting a mortgage for £100,000 you simply take possession of the property and then repay the seller at an agreed rate over an agreed period at an agreed amount. So you pay your monthly 'mortgage' to the seller rather than to the finance company. In this case you have had complete seller financing, and the added bonus here is that you have also taken possession of this property without putting any of your own money into the deal.

If you think that this is too good to be true, rest assured that this is going on in the UK each and every day many, many times. There are many people who have built up their entire property portfolio of many millions of pounds purely by purchasing properties from sellers who provide the finance. It is, for instance, a very popular method with elderly (and knowledgeable) property owners, particularly if they are selling their house to provide a regular income or pension.

In fact, my Dad bought his first house in exactly this way from his Dad. Just after the war in 1948 when Mum and Dad were expecting my elder brother and they needed somewhere to live, Grandad owned a property in the East End of London but lived elsewhere. So my Dad bought the house from Grandad at an agreed price of a few hundred pounds. They had a little red book and every week Grandad would come round and collect from Dad the agreed amount. They noted the amounts in the little red book and eventually the house was bought – completely on seller financing.

GIFTED OR GHOSTED DEPOSITS

Now this is a more complicated method of financing property purchases and the method that confuses many to a greater or lesser degree. How does it work?

Let's say we have the same property being sold for £100,000. In this case however, we are buying this property at a discount.

Again, most people worry too much about why this might be the case, but just imagine that there are some people out there who want to deal in property at 'wholesale' prices, and those who want to deal at retail prices. It is easy to understand why people buy T-shirts at wholesale prices and then sell them on at retail prices, so just think of properties as T-shirts. Some people buy property at wholesale prices and then sell on to the public at retail. The task in this particular scenario is to buy direct from a property wholesaler.

So in this case the seller is selling a property at £100,000 which is the true open market value of the property, but he has agreed to sell it to me at a discount at £90,000. In this case, if I can get a mortgage based on open market value i.e. the £100,000 rather than the purchase price of £90,000, I can obtain the property with none of my own money. So, I get a mortgage for £90,000 based on 90% of the open market value of the property, which I then pay over to the seller on completion day. If I obtain £90,000 in finance and the selling price is £90,000 – clearly I have not put any money into the deal.

In this case the extra 10% has been generated only by the difference between the selling price and the market value.

Clearly though this scheme only works if you are buying properties at below market – or at wholesale – prices. And of course, the finance provider needs to be happy with this valuation versus market price type of deal.

This is yet another version of the no money down deals you have heard or read about. Does it happen in reality? Yes it does frequently and regularly.

It is known as a ghosted deposit arrangement because no deposit effectively ever exists – it's an apparition!

These deals are quoted very much in the more excitable investment magazines, but you need to be clear that the mortgage is raised based on the open market value of the property rather than the purchase price – some finance providers like this and some don't. In general, the American type of providers are happier with it as it is more common in the United States.

It is also very common to see these deals with new build properties, when the developer will advertise that there is a 5% or 10% deposit paid. They never intend to give you money as a wheel barrow of used notes – they do it exactly as described above – with a ghosted deposit.

Please be aware that these deals are unusual and you and your team need to be comfortable with it. Some advisers and solicitors will warn against these deals due to mortgage fraud and if they do, you need to ask them to explain what they mean, but in simple terms, these deals do constitute mortgage fraud but only IF you artificially inflate the purchase price above that of the market in order to generate a false value on which to base your mortgage.

These whole transactions can take place with no money (except for legal and incidental expenses) being paid by the purchaser: another genuine no money down deal.

CASH BACK DEALS

CASH OUT OR CASH BACK AT COMPLETION

Level one

Now let us start this next topic by continuing with a similar example to the one we had in the last section on gifted deposits. If the property in question had been valued at, say £150,000 but was being sold (wholesale) at £130,000, you will see that actually there is spare money left over at completion.

If the purchaser goes through all the steps above for gifted deposits and also obtains a 90% mortgage for the property, the purchaser will obtain 90% of £150,000 – being £135,000 - from the finance house, but only £130,000 is due to the seller. So on completion day there is £5,000 left over to pay for all the costs and to give the purchaser some cash back at completion.

Again, does it actually ever happen? The answer again is yes although the deals will be harder to find.

Level two

The example above related purely to a normal purchase of a property to be vacated on completion, but let us think about what happens when the property is already tenanted and when the tenants will stay in residence after completion of the sale of the property.

On exchange of contracts for this purchase, we may agree to pay a deposit to the current owner or we may come to some other arrangement for seller financing or gifted deposits. However, let us say that just for this example we pay a deposit of £5,000 on exchange of contracts. This deposit we pay with a bank overdraft or flexible loan, or possibly even a credit card. So what are the numbers?

1 We exchange contracts putting our £5,000 deposit into the solicitors.

2 Some time later we get to completion day. Let us just assume for simplicity that completion takes place on the 1st of the month.

3 At that time we receive:

a) the months rent from the tenant in advance.

b) the tenant's deposits or bonds from the existing landlord.

So as long as the total of the rents plus the tenants deposits are greater than our £5,000 deposit, we have cash in hand – or cash back at completion.

Clearly, the figures used here are simplified to make the explanation as straight forward as possible, but you can see that the principle works, and you can now start to look for these type of deals at your local auction house (find your local auction by searching on www.ukpad.com), or on the internet or from your usual property sourcing agent.

Before we finish on this particular section there are four points to clear up:

1 The ongoing income stream. In most cases the monthly payment out to the mortgage provider will not happen until the 1st of the next month. One glorious cash flow advantage of these strategies is that rent is payable monthly in advance and mortgages generally are payable monthly in arrears. So we will have the first months rent and the second months rent before we need to pay our first mortgage payment.

2 What happens if we complete mid month, or part way through the month? This is fine too, and in fact in some cases this is even better. In normal mid month transaction, all that happens is that the rents due are time apportioned between the two owners, being the seller and the purchaser of the property. So, you need to check the figures for each specific example that you find. And of course, there will also be a time apportioned mortgage payment to be made. OR maybe not! Some mortgage providers do not even collect part month payments but chose instead to hold collection of monies until their normal DD run date.

So let's say that we complete on the 7th of the month but the bank providing the money does their normal collection on the 1st. If you complete on the 7th September, it is likely that your first mortgage payment will not be due until 1st NOVEMBER, rather than the 1st October.

In this case you can ask the finance provider to charge you the additional interest incurred on the money at the next mortgage collection day. So your first mortgage payment will be higher than normal, and will represent one full month of interest plus interest for the period of 7th September to 1st October.

Or in some cases you can ask for the extra interest to be added to the principal of the loan rather than being collected as a payment. It will normally make a difference to the overall amount owed of only a few hundred pounds over 25 (or more) years.

The outcome of all these variations is to boost your cash flow, so that you get more money at the beginning, generally when you need it most, so it is worth exploring all the options.

3 What happens to the tenant's deposits? Obviously, in the fullness of time the tenant's deposits will need to be returned to them or passed to the next owner of the property. But at the moment the law allows you to hold minimal deposits yourself, so you can keep these deposits and return them only at the end of the tenancy. In this instance you have had the use of the money for the whole time. In most cases the return payment of the outgoing tenants deposit is met by the incoming tenant's deposit and advance rental.

4 What happens to the interest on the deposit of £5,000 paid on the credit card or on loan? The interest payable on the deposit for a month would be repaid out of the excess funds generated on completion. OR, if you had put this deposit on a credit card cheque you could have repaid it within 28 days with the funds from completion and possibly paid no interest or charges at all. OR, even better, if exchange and completion had been on the same day (perfectly possible and quite normal) you would not have had to fund the £5,000 at all. Yet another no money down deal!

TOP TIP

The amount you pay as deposit on any property is purely an agreement between the seller and the buyer. If you both agree that the deposit should be 5% or 2% or even 0%, it's entirely up to the two people concerned. Also a deposit can be provided from an insurance policy rather than cash – so you pay an insurance premium of a few pounds rather than a deposit of many thousands.

CASH BACK DEALS

Level three

Another way of getting cash back at completion is to do back-to-back property transactions. This involves selling a property effectively at the same time as you buy it. This is how it works:

1 You see a property that you think might be undervalued, at say, £80,000. You think it could probably get £90,000 if the property was advertised correctly.

2 You make an offer for the property at £80,000, and the deal goes ahead with you exchanging contracts for completion on the 1st of July.

3 You then advertise the property for sale at £90,000 (or anywhere in between £80,000 to £90,000) with one condition – that completion takes place on the 1st July.

4 You get a buyer and you exchange contracts.

5 On the 1st of July you buy the property at £80,000 as agreed.

6 A few hours later you sell the property for £90,000.

7 You never move in, you just act as a property broker. All you have done is matched a buyer and a seller, with you in the middle taking the £10,000 profit.

8 You get the £10,000 out at completion as cash from the solicitor.

9 Apart from fees, which you have fixed in advance, your costs have been minimal.

These are super deals but remember you need two things:

a) A solicitor with a strong heart beat! – as they can get concerned doing this on the same day. It might be better if you leave a day or two between the buy and the sell transaction.

b) A different sort of financing. Clearly you do not need a 25 year mortgage for this transaction. A short term overdraft is more appropriate, so speak to your bank.

This type of transaction is often used when buying off plan, or buying to plan whereby you reserve a property on a new development whilst the buildings are still at plan stage. You fix your price for purchase with the building development company, and once the property completion date is fixed, you then can go and find a buyer for 'your' property, obviously at a higher price. It is usual to see prices rise during the building stage and particularly if the development is well marketed by the development company, you can often get a substantial premium for the property just by being in the deal at the early stage.

Clearly you would have to fund a deposit at some stage with both these back-to-back strategies. However, you can agree a small deposit or zero deposit if possible and it is common for building development companies to fund deposits or refund deposits or give some other cash back incentive that should lessen the blow. Also remember that before exchange you can often secure first refusal on new developments with a minimal 'fee' of a few hundred pounds, which is normally refundable anyway if you do not go ahead with the purchase.

TOP TIP You can get an even better deal if you purchase new development properties but 'assign' them on before you become the full owner. In some circumstances you can even pass the stamp duty payable onto the new buyer – making the deal even better for you.

No money down deals

Most people are captivated by how they can buy property with no money, and the simplest way is just to get a mortgage for 100% of the purchase price.

What has happened here is that you have bought the property with none of YOUR money down at all, and that is what genuine no money down deals are – they are purely deals when you arrange the financing such that you don't actually part with any of your own money from your bank, purse or wallet.

Much has been written to glamourise the no money down deal but it is really a very basic and ordinary scheme that happens with different variations.

No money down deals can be broken down into three categories: the first is genuine no money down EVER type deals and we have already seen some of those. The second type is a "no money down out of my pocket at the moment", and the final type is a "no money down EVENTUALLY" deal.

When you read about no money down deals you will find that the vast majority of the schemes illustrated are methods of manipulation of some kind of personal debt, and they are in the main credit card arrangements.

But let us just run through some of the other types of no money down deal first and then we can address the credit card game.

So, no money down can be when:

1   You get a 100% mortgage

2   You get 100% funding for a property from a combination of a mortgage or seller financing.

3   You get 100% seller financing.

4   You get a gifted deposit from the seller and get a mortgage for the rest.

5   You use the family silver (or some other asset) as the deposit for the property. Clearly the seller has to agree to receive an asset other than money as a deposit.

6   You get a personal loan, or overdraft in combination with a mortgage.

7   You use your credit card (or variety of credit cards) to top up the mortgage to the purchase amount.

And as an example of the third type of no money down eventually deal you can buy a property, refurbish it and then re-mortgage it at a higher value and consequently withdraw all your original investment at the end.

An illustration might be to:
Buy a distressed property for £50,000 using a 90% loan to value, £45,000 mortgage and a £5,000 loan. Then spend another £3,000 refurbishing the property using credit cards. Then, when the property is looking good go back to the finance provider and ask them to revalue it. Let's say that they re-value it at £60,000. Then apply for a new mortgage at the higher re-valued amount, and at 90% loan to value they now provide a mortgage of £54,000. It is now possible to repay the original loan of £45,000 and have £9,000 left over to clear the loan debt of £5,000 (used for the deposit) AND the £3,000 refurbishment costs – and also have £1,000 left over. Although there is money invested along the way, this deal has been completed with no money down eventually, and is covered in more detail later in this section.

TOP TIP

If you intend to do this kind of refurbishment strategy be careful to arrange the original finance with re-valuation in mind. Some finance providers do this willingly, some will only re-value after a given period and some don't like this at all. If this is a main part of your strategy include some questions about their approach to re-valuations at an early stage.

Now let's look at credit cards more closely with an example.

Credit cards have become amazingly flexible and you can obtain huge amounts of information if you look at web sites such as:
www.moneysupermarket.com
www.uk-credit-cards-online.co.uk
www.thisismoney.co.uk (look in the money shop section).

You can see, analyse and search for credit cards in a multitude of ways. You can see those that have 0% on balance transfers, those with 0% interest for a given period, those with annual fees and those without.

For the purpose of this example, let us say that you have applied and received two credit cards: one a Visa and one a Master card. You have also seen a property for £50,000.

a) You obtain a mortgage for say, 90% of the value, being £45,000.

b) You put the deposit of £5,000 on credit card number 1; let's say it's the Visa card.

c) 28 days or so later the Visa Company write to you with a statement and ask for their £5,000 back.

d) At that stage you get the nice people who have given you a MasterCard to write a cheque to Visa for £5,000.

e) You clear the Visa balance.

f) 28 days or so later, MasterCard ask for their £5,000 back, at which point you get the nice people at Visa to pay the £5,000 over to MasterCard.

g) And then 28 days or so later Visa write to you again, and so on and so on......

The £5,000 deposit swings back and forth like a pendulum between the two credit cards and you can do this until you either can afford to pay it off, or you get the property re-valued at an increased value such that your new 90% mortgage provides enough money to pay the £5,000 off.

The credit card companies are quite used to this type of behaviour and will even automatically transfer the money back and forth for you, so you don't even have to bother writing cheques!

Obviously, if these are normal credit cards, there will be interest accruing – but only if you don't get the payment in on time. So you should be able to keep the pendulum swinging with careful planning and timing. If not, you may have to pay some interest.

Careful selection of credit cards is the key to this particular strategy. It is clearly easier to have credit cards that will give you:
• credit card cheques
• 0% interest on balance transfers, and
• 0% on new purchases.

It is also preferable to get the 0% on balance transfers for as long a period as possible – it is usually 6 months or so, but there have been occasions when credit card companies have made this period much longer – even in one case, 0% balance transfer rate was for the life of the balance!

The other version of this is to take 6 months interest free credit on cards 1 and 2, and when those 6 months is up apply for cards 3 and 4, and use them for 6 months and then get cards 5 and 6, and so on.

Obviously, if you have a credit card that gives you a straight forward interest free period for six months, you can just leave the deposit on that card for the whole of the six months and then swing the pendulum, and move the balance to an additional card.

To make this work you may still need two credit cards; one that gives you credit card cheques (and most do) and one that gives you an interest free period on balance transfers for, say, six months. So use the credit card cheque to pay the deposit on the property and when the credit card payment is due, and then transfer the balance on to the card with 0% interest on balance transfers. There may be a small fee to pay for the credit card cheque itself, but if you clear the balance by the due date the effect of this will be negligible. By careful planning of exchange and completion dates you can maximise the credit free periods and available credit. So even on a one month cycle, the due date may be anything up to 56 days away – so chose your completion dates carefully to gain that extra month of interest freedom!

NO MONEY DOWN - EVENTUALLY

All the no money down deals so far have concentrated on there being no money down at the beginning. These techniques are so popular because:

- often people don't have any money when they get started

- although payments may eventually have to be made, in many cases financial outlay can be deferred for many years until other cash and other wealth has been generated.

However, there are another selection of no money down deals where they actually mean 'no money down – eventually'!

Now this is not so attractive for those people who do not have any starting capital but can actually be a very successful and wealth generating proposition. Let's run through an example.

Let's say I find a property sourcing agent who works in a specific area of the country where properties are less expensive. Let's say that in reality the capital growth opportunities are not as high as they might be in other parts of the country, but the income potential is high and relatively secure.

So the agent finds a property that is 'distressed' and needs attention and consequently is being sold below market value. You buy that and then have the property renovated. It is important to be very careful here about the level of 'distress' of the property. In order for this strategy to work most efficiently the level of renovation needed needs to be cosmetic only. Structural damage may work financially and may generate sufficient returns, but it takes much longer to complete the work and there may be more risks involved. If you want to do this strategy on structurally distressed property make sure that you include a longer time period in your calculations.

When the refurbishment of the property is completed and 'squeaky clean' you then have it re-valued. Of course, it is then valued at a higher price than you bought it, and if you have chosen the right property, you can at that stage get all your money back.

So let's say you buy a run down property for £20,000 and spend £5,000 refurbishing it. At that stage it is re-valued at £30,000. You apply for a mortgage at 85% of loan to value, and get a mortgage for £25,500. At that stage you get back your initial outlay of £20,000, your costs of £5,000 plus £500 as a contribution to your expenses. In addition, you now own 15% (i.e. 100% - 85% mortgage) in a property that you didn't have before!

Finance note

Some finance providers will not provide loans or mortgages for below £25,000 – and some will – so if you are looking at this strategy, and you want to be able to get a mortgage on the increased value at the end of the day, then you need to evaluate whether the re-valued amount will be £25,000 or more.
Or find a finance provider that is happy to work below £25,000.

The added spice

Even though this simple strategy of buy, do up and revalue, is very attractive – it gets even better than that. This technique can be the starting point in a variety of property investment strategies. So consider at this stage:

1 Taking out the money at the end of the first refurbishment and re-investing it in another property, and then another, and another. In a very short time, you will own 15% (or a different percentage dependant on the mortgage you get) of lots of properties.

2 The income option. Each property, if it is properly managed could produce a regular income. So if you got a tenant in each property as you acquired it, you could get a rental of, let's say £80 per week. This equates to £347 per calendar month. The monthly cost of the mortgage of £25,500 (as above) would be approximately £125. On these rough calculations, each of these properties would then produce over £200 per month income.

So, let's summarise where we are: you have made an initial investment of £25,000 which is used to purchase a string of properties all generating a net cash inflow of approximately £200 per month. So even if you had borrowed the initial £25,000 on a personal loan, you would still be cash positive at the end of the day, and you would be accumulating self funding assets, at whatever pace you wanted.

That same £25,000 can be rolled over and rolled over and rolled over until you want to stop acquiring properties.

TOP TIP

Think about two or more of the strategies above together to create a fantastic property investment portfolio. It would be possible to follow the strategy above that rolled over the same initial investment into a succession of properties – with the added bonus of the initial investment being on the credit card pendulum system. So, you accumulate properties that somebody else funds on a monthly basis from rental income and the whole lot is acquired with no money down. Double whammy!

And then, even if you just left all these properties to accumulate at small rates of capital growth per year, for the full 25 years of the mortgage, by the time you retired (or in any case, in 25 years) you will have a selection of income generating assets that you have accumulated that someone else (i.e. the tenants) have paid for.

Nice work!

CREDIT MANAGEMENT

It is important to note that before you start any strategy involving revolving credit of any kind, particularly if you are using credit cards, is to make sure that your credit rating is going to survive the process.

Every time you make any application for a credit card, personal loan, hire purchase or whatever, it leaves a 'footprint' on your credit file. Now this may not be a bad thing, but you need to be careful not to go charging in applying for 6 credit cards all at once, because this might look odd on your credit file.

There are also companies who may refuse credit purely on a given number of 'footprints' on the file – even if they were just credit checks rather than credit approvals.

TOP TIP

Watch this issue when applying for multiple mortgages. If you can get one lender to provide you with a block of ten mortgages, this leaves a much better trail on your credit file than applying for ten mortgages with ten different providers. Another possibility is to apply for a line of credit rather than specific mortgages. So apply for, say £250,000 for a maximum of 6 properties, as one application – shop around and you will find mortgage providers happy to do this.

Credit checking

You can see your own credit file and how it is impacted by your financial behaviours by contacting a credit monitoring company such as: Experian or Equifax. If you go onto their web sites: www.experian.co.uk, or www.equifax.co.uk, you will be able to apply for your own credit file. It will only cost a few pounds and in a few days you will receive a complete information pack about you and your money.

Alternatively for between £20 and £40 you can subscribe to an agency such as www.checkmyfile.com that will send you regular credit file checks.

When you see the information you will be able to understand how best to use the information and how to alter it. There are many things you can do with your credit history, including change it or improve it, so it is well worth looking at this now and then checking it periodically for changes.

It is worth checking many credit checking companies when you first start because they each provide slightly different information, and then just use the one you like best for ongoing checks.

If you are going to embark on no money down strategies for property finance that involves credit, then you need to take personal responsibility for your credit history and reporting.

If you have any odd or false information on your file you can get it removed, and even if there are some genuine 'black marks' on file, you can help yourself by explaining these in advance to credit providers.

If you are in any doubt about credit please speak to a debt counsellor, who you can find through your local citizens advice bureau, or look for consumer credit advisers on the internet.

The Credit Card Challenge

As a final reminder in this section on creative financing deals, remember to regularly update your credit position with credit cards. Clearly we shouldn't try to increase credit every day, but schedule in a six monthly review of your credit cards where you can then increase your limits and reduce interest rates.

When you call your credit card remember to ask for RSPCA:

Rate

What rate am I charged?
Can you reduce it please?

Special deals

Do you have any 0% deals available for me?
What other special offers do you have?
Do you have a better deal for me at the moment?

Pay annual fee

Is there an annual fee?
Can you waive it please? Or reduce it please?

Credit limit

What is the credit limit?
Can you increase it?
When can you increase it?

Any specials?

Can I have the new deal?
The new card? The Black Card?
The Elite Package? What's new?

Always remember that every time you get a no or blocking answer from any financial provider – ask them "what would I have to do in order to get what I need?" and often the finance provider will tell you exactly what to do – so you get your own personal financial action plan.

INTRODUCTION TO FINANCIAL EVALUATION

There are many ways to financially evaluate the property deal you are looking at and at this stage it is best that you think very clearly about your overall strategy for purchasing. The type of strategy that you are implementing will determine the evaluation method you chose. So if you have an income generating strategy clearly you need an income or yield type evaluation method. If your strategy is a capital one, then the yield figure may be completely irrelevant.

So start with the end in mind and then keep your evaluation as simple as possible – as long as you use your method consistently then you are fine.

Consider each of the following points in respect of your own proposed property strategy:

1 How are you going to support yourself? (and possibly your family?)

If you decide to take the option to stay in paid employment and accumulate properties in the background to act as a pension for your retirement income, you may not want your properties to generate income, because if you do the tax man will take some away! In this situation the ideal evaluation method is to ensure that all property investments generate a zero net return i.e. an income of nothing! In this case you get the properties at retirement but there has not been any income tax to pay throughout the whole time that the properties have been accumulating.

Or you may have the choice to give up the job and live off the property income, in which case it is highly imperative that you get high income producing assets and therefore to evaluate each property on its income potential is vital. Some people might want a mix of income and capital growth in which case a mix of evaluation methods may work.

2 What is your investment strategy?

What is the investment strategy for each property, and by that you need to consider what you want to do with the property once you have it! Here we may want to consider if it is: a buy to let (income): a buy to hold (capital): a buy-to refurbish-to sell (capital); a buy-to refurbish-to let (capital + income), and so on.

Clearly for each type of exit strategy we need to consider a different financial evaluation. Any property that needs refurbishment requires you to be aware of costs, materials and labour. Buying already tenanted properties, on the other hand, provides an immediate income with no additional outlay.

TOP TIP
Ask yourself why you are dong this and then find a financial evaluation tool that fits your investment strategy. If you have more than one strategy in play, then have more than one financial evaluation tool.

FINANCIAL EVALUATION: SOME OF THE METHODS

There are as many different ways of evaluating property investments as there are different properties: it is vital to find the method that works for you. Some evaluation tools are very complex and some very simple. It is more important to find one that you are comfortable with and that you can apply consistently and easily, than it is to evaluate properties with complicated systems that are onerous to complete.

In all cases below I have used the term 'property cost' as one item, but remember that when you evaluate property cost include the costs of:

- The property

- The survey (if you have one)

- The valuers fees (probably required by your financial provider)

- Stamp duty

- Solicitors or conveyancing costs

- Finance arrangement fees

- Any other initial costs.

Stamp Duty

Stamp duty is a variable amount payable on the purchase of assets such as shares and property. Currently in the UK for property it varies from 0% to 4% on a sliding scale on properties valued at £60,000 or more. Check the Inland Revenue web site: www.inlandrevenue.gov.uk for the latest rates applicable.

NB There are some stamp duty exemptions available for purchase of property in certain designated disadvantaged areas – see www.inlandrevenue.gov.uk/rates/stamprates.htm for further information and a list of the areas concerned.

TOP TIP

The stamp duty rates across Europe are generally higher than they are in the UK. In Ireland for example, stamp duty can be as high as 9% so be prepared for equalisation of these rates in the future, if the UK joins monetary forces with the EU.

FINANCIAL EVALUATION OF CAPITAL STRATEGIES

1 The gross capital gain percentage.

To calculate your total capital gain percentage deduct the purchase cost from the sales proceeds to get a capital gain figure. Express this gain as a percentage of your investment. If you set yourself a percentage target to achieve, use that target as the tool by which you determine which properties to buy, and those properties that don't make the grade are eliminated from your potential purchasing pool, and those that make the grade, get moved onto be further evaluated.

So, let's say a property costs: £100,000

We sell it for: £120,000

Making a capital gain of: £ 20,000

Which expressed as a percentage of the cost of £100,000 is:

£20,000/£100,000 x 100 20%

If you have set your target gain at 10%, this property makes the cut, and if your target is set at 50% it doesn't!

TOP TIP

If you are using this method try setting your capital gain target as a relation of your cost of capital. So if you can borrow money at 10%, you may think that anything over 10% is a winner, but perhaps think about targeting your potential gain to be, say, twice your cost of capital.

2 Gross return including the total cost of refurbishment

If you are buying to refurbish to re-sell you need to include all the costs of renovation.

So, if a property costs: £60,000

We spend on refurbishment: £15,000

We sell it for: £95,000

Making a capital gain of: £20,000

Which expressed as a percentage of the total cost of £75,000 is:

£20,000/£75,000 x 100 26.67%

For evaluation purposes consider if 26.67% is meeting your target or not and your decision is then easily made.

TOP TIP

Develop a comprehensive refurbishment cost control list as part of your evaluation tool kit. DON'T FORGET to include a cost for the time it takes to renovate and allow for costs during that time: allow for the mortgage, council and water taxes, service charges and other costs in your evaluation.

3 Cash flow method: capital purchases

If your strategy is to invest in property for capital growth, the financial evaluation you need is to ask "can I afford to support it"? In this case list all the outgoings to give you a cash outflow figure per month. Feed this outflow figure into your normal monthly budgeted expenditure as you would the costs of a home you lived in. Remember to include the costs of such things as:

- Mortgage

- Insurances

- Council Tax

- Water standing charges

- Basic gas and or electricity charges

- Telephone

- General maintenance and repairs.

In addition, you may wish to do a sensitivity analysis with this and play 'what if'. You can take the basics costs as outlined above – or amended for your own personal circumstances – and test each cost:

- if the interest rate rose by 1%, or 2% or even 10% does the investment still work?

- or how much would the interest rate have to rise before the investment no longer worked?

- is there enough gain in the property to afford a major repair such as the roof needing replacement?

- does the investment still work if there were a managing agent looking after the property?

- how much would your circumstances have to change before the investment became a financial burden rather than a gift? Consider loss of jobs, getting divorced, having that 17th grandchild!

- if there was a sudden influx of money – such as winning the lottery would the investment still work?

This final question is one that is most pertinent because it forces you to really challenge the success of the investment in terms of the strategy and the longer term position. If you ask yourself this question the type of answer you have includes:

- still keep the property investment and use the inheritance for other things (which confirms the relevance, and success of the original investment decision)

- confirm that there is no better use – or better return - than the property (which again confirms the original investment decision)

- pay off this mortgage immediately (which perhaps suggests a lack of confidence in the original investment strategy), or

- use the inheritance money to get out the investment altogether (in which case, oops – perhaps we had the strategy wrong in the first place!).

FINANCIAL EVALUATION OF INCOME SCHEMES

With income strategies, clearly you have some target
in mind for income generation, so what is it?

Some ways to evaluate income are as
follows:

1   Cash flow basis

In this evaluation you just take all the inflows
and deduct all the outflows and see what is left.

	Per month ££
Rental income	....
Less:	
Funding costs	....
Insurances	....
Management fees	....
Gas and safety costs	....
Other costs	....
Net cash inflow/outflow	_____

When you evaluate in this way make sure that you include the costs that are relevant to you and your investment strategy. So for example, if you are going to manage all your investment properties yourself, including finding tenants, and collecting rents then you do not need to include an allowance for any management fees. However, if you need to delegate all the management because the property is at the other end of the country and you never intend to ever go there, then clearly you need to allocate a far greater proportion of costs to its management.

Also check specific management fees as they vary across the country, and there is usually a higher charge for student type properties than a professional let. Also bear in mind that the more properties you have the greater your bargaining power with agents.

Once you get to the net cash inflow/outflow stage above you then set your financial target. Do you just want this to be zero or at best plus £1? Or do you want this to be £100 per month, £200 or more?

If you have several properties, think also about how this specific investment fits into the rest of your property investment portfolio. Do you want your properties to be cash positive overall, in which case you may be able to include properties (for some other reason perhaps) that are not immediately cash positive, because somewhere else in the portfolio there is another property that generates sufficient cash per month to offset the losses on other properties.

Then consider other costs. These will vary from person to person and from strategy to strategy. For example, you can get maintenance contracts for anything and everything that you will need: gas boiler annual checks, normal gas and electricity maintenance, plumbing, cleaning, redecorating, carpet cleaning and so on. One approach would be to include the costs of maintenance contracts for all these things – and hence reduce your monthly cash flow. OR, you may be a less prudent personality and you are happy to take the hit of specific costs when they occur.

Only you will know what is the right level of cash flow for you and your particular strategy, and you can adjust your evaluation accordingly to suit your circumstances.

TOP TIP Always remember that you can insure anything and everything that is connected with rental properties – in fact you can now even insure against void periods!

FINANCIAL EVALUATION OF INCOME SCHEMES

2 Gross return basis

This is a fairly simple but effective method as it takes your gross return as a percentage of the purchase cost as follows:

Take the monthly rent x 12 months:	Annual rent
Take the annual rent/purchase price x 100	Gross return per year
So rent of £750 per month, equates to: £750 x 12:	£9,000
Say the property cost:	£75,000
Take: £9,000/£75,000 x 100:	12%

With this gross return you can then ask yourself questions like:

- what is the cost of funding that I will pay when I invest in this property? (if it is less than 12% then it looks positive, but if it is more than 12% then ask if this property is right for you?)

- what else could I do with the money that may generate more than 12%? (if you have several other opportunities here, don't invest in the property: if no then continue to evaluate the property positively).

TOP TIP

Practice playing with this type of formula and you will soon get familiar with calculations, and as a minimum use these figures to compare one potential investment against another, to evaluate the best property for you.

3   Net annual profit basis

This method will provide you with a net profit or loss percentage which you can evaluate as if it were any other business.

So take the cash inflows less the outflows to leave a residual monthly balance. Multiply that by 12 months to get an annualised profit figure. Express that figure as a percentage of the gross income, to get the net profit per year.

	££
Monthly rental income	....
Less:	
Monthly funding costs	....
Other monthly costs	....
Tax	....
Net monthly inflow/outflow	_____

Take this net figure and multiply by 12 to get an annual profit.
Take the annual profit and divide it by the gross annual rent (the rental income x 12) and then multiply by 100.
This will give you an annual profit percentage.

Let's say the annual inflow is £4,500,
and the annual rental is £9,000 (£750 x 12).
Our annual profit percentage is: £4,500/£9,000 x 100 = 50%

This will then give you a figure that you can evaluate against other business opportunities, and other property investments.

> **TOP TIP**
>
> Make sure that you include fully all the costs you may incur, and again these will be different for each of you and will depend on your personal level of input to the management of the properties.

4   Return on cash invested or cash on cash invested

This is probably the most common method of evaluating property investments. It is calculated by taking the net cash inflow - as above – and expressing that as a percentage of the amount of money YOU have invested in the property. After all, you are only really interested in what return you get on your funds. (Clearly this evaluation method doesn't work if you have done a 'no money down' deal!).

So if the net inflow is £4,500 on a property that cost £100,000 and you put down a 10% deposit of £10,000,
the calculation is: £4,500/£10,000 x 100   45%

Once again the questions you ask at this stage are the same: what better use do you have for the money? How does this compare to other businesses and other property investments?

Rest assured that after you have done these calculations a few times you will become very quick and adept and making the calculations quickly and on the back of an envelope as you are viewing properties.

> **TOP TIP**
>
> Create for yourself a property review pack which has as many of these evaluation methods as you want to use. If you have blank forms available you can create a simple and quick system of property evaluation.

FINANCIAL EVALUATION OF MORTGAGE TYPES

Finally, before we leave the evaluation section, let's consider some basic calculations on mortgage types and amounts. Using a very simple example we can prove some basic financial rules to ourselves.

ILLUSTRATION

We have a fictional property which is being sold for £100,000. It has a tenant in it paying £750 per month rent.

Proposal 1 – repayment mortgage:

We purchase the property and we obtain an 80% loan to value **standard repayment** mortage of £80,000 at 5%. What is our cash on cash return?

	£
Rent	750
Less:	
Mortgage payments	473
Management fee	75
Other costs, say	75
Net monthly cash flow	127

Our annual return is therefore £127 x 12 months = £1,524

Our return is therefore £1,524 expressed as a percentage of OUR money invested - £20,000 (being the deposit of 20%).

£1,524/£20,000 x 100 = 7.6%

Proposal 2 – 80% interest only mortgage:

We purchase the property and we obtain an 80% loan to value **interest only** mortgage of £80,000 at 5%. What is our cash on cash return?

	£
Rent	750
Less:	
Mortgage payments	334
Management fee	75
Other costs, say	75
Net monthly cash flow	266

Our annual return is therefore £266 x 12 months = £3,192

Our return is therefore £3,192 expressed as a percentage of OUR money invested - £20,000 (being the deposit of 20%).

£3,192/£20,000 x 100 = 15.9%

Immediately we can see with this simple example that interest only mortgages have two great benefits: firstly we get much more cash from the property each month, and the return on our own invested cash is much higher.

[But don't forget that with interest only mortgages you still have to repay the capital sum at the end – so review the notes above on strategies for that].

Proposal 3 – 85% interest only mortgage:

We purchase the property and we obtain an **interest only**, larger mortgage of 85% loan to value of £85,000 at 5%. What is our cash on cash return?

	£
Rent	750
Less:	
Mortgage payments	354
Management fee	75
Other costs, say	75
Net monthly cash flow	246

Our annual return is therefore £246 x 12 months = £2,952

Our return is therefore £2,952 expressed as a percentage of OUR money invested – which is now lower at £15,000 (being the deposit of 15%).

£2,952/£15,000 x 100 = 19.7%

This proposal 3 gives us the highest return on our money of all three examples, and yet we have invested the least!

It is because: the smaller our cash investment, the higher the percentage returns, because we are using other people's money!

NB The mortgage quotes used in each of the three proposals were taken from What Mortgage magazine.

FINANCIAL EVALUATION OF BOTH INCOME AND CAPITAL STRATEGIES

Property Comparables Sheet

Before you finally decide to purchase the property always do a comparable analysis. Find at least five other properties that are comparable to the property being evaluated. They need to be as close a comparison as possible in terms of location, position, size, and condition. Please note special or distinguishing features.

These properties can be found from the internet, agencies, auction catalogues or your own database.

Property One:
Value (and rental if relevant)   £.............

                                                  £.............

Property Two:
Value (and rental if relevant)   £.............

                                                  £.............

Property Three:
Value (and rental if relevant)   £.............

                                                  £.............

Property Four:
Value (and rental if relevant)   £.............

                                                  £.............

Property Five:
Value (and rental if relevant)   £.............

                                                  £.............

Summary averages for the 5 above

                     £.............   £.............

Compared to:

The property being evaluated:

Value (and rental if relevant)   £.............   £.............

So, does it compare favourably or not?

The Lease Option Purchase

Now thanks to the press and the media generally, the buy to let property investment is now well known and well understood, but what about let-to-buy? It is a very simple process that is used commonly in the United States, and is catching on very fast in the UK. It is the purchase of a lease option, and the lease option contract that we will now go through is perfectly legal in the UK.

So let's imagine that you want to buy a property but you have no money. You have a poor or damaged credit rating and no method of raising loans, deposits or even the transaction costs but yet you want to buy a property. You can do it through a lease option.

This is how it works.

You see a property for sale at £50,000. The mortgage on that particular property at 100% would cost approximately £250 per month. You have a regular monthly income but nothing else. You can afford to pay perhaps £450 per month for it. You estimate that it will take you two years to repair your credit at which time you fully expect to be able to get an appropriate mortgage. For simplicity in this example, we will also assume that the capital growth on this property is 10% per year.

So you approach the current owner and propose the following:

1   That you agree to purchase the property on a lease option whereby you buy the property at a given date, say two years in the future (when your credit is repaired).

2   That you agree to pay £450 per month for the two years you live there before the option is taken up – or exercised.

3   You agree the future price.

Now this might by anything at all. Some people might fix the price at today's price, i.e. £50,000. Some people might allow for some capital growth – so at 10% per annum capital growth, this property would be worth £60,500 in two years time. So it is most likely that you would agree an amount between these two figures – to allow some discount for the purchaser and to allow some profit for the seller. For this example we can assume a figure of £55,000

4   You agree that of the £450 you pay per month of which, say, £115 per month is a down payment for the deposit on the property in two years' time.

5   After two years, you have paid £115 per month for two years, making a total of £2,760 as a deposit, which equates to just over 5% of the agreed purchase price of £55,000.

6   At the end of the two years and when the option matures the property is worth £60,500, and with your repaired credit you easily get a mortgage for £52,240 (being £55,000 less £2,760 – the deposit paid on instalments), as this represents only 86% of the market value at the time.

So what has happened for the seller of the property?

1   The seller has a guaranteed buyer for the property.

2   The seller has a careful and motivated tenant who is very unlikely to trash the property.

3   In the meantime, the seller is collecting £450 per month, which pays the mortgage of £250, allows £115 as a part payment against the future deposit, and – great news – the seller then gets a further £85 per month for doing absolutely nothing.

4   The seller gets the cash flow benefit of the £115 each month to use elsewhere.

5   The eventual sales price allows for some profit on the original investment – the growth is only 5% per year but it is guaranteed.

6   If the purchaser then doesn't want the property in two years at the option maturity time (which is the purchasers option), the seller then has the added benefit of a windfall bonus of £2,760 – the deposit which has been accumulated and which is now forfeited.

7   AND – the seller can now go and sell their property for £60,500 as well.

What has happened for the buyer of the property?

1 The buyer has a guaranteed place to live for two years, which they like and hope to own.

2 The buyer has a seller who accepts the deposit in stage payments.

3 The buyer has two years to sort out their credit rating.

4 The buyer gets a property at a discount of 5% in two years' time.

5 In two years and starting from a position of having absolutely nothing, the buyer has their own home.

This is a total win-win for both parties

So what about the professional property investor?

The scenario above is very nice and heart warming, but the process can work for any property transaction, whether you are the buyer or the seller. You will all be able to see situations where you might be able to take advantage of this scheme from one side or the other.

Furthermore, you may actually get experienced enough to manipulate these options by being a piggy in the middle. So, using the example above, assume that you are the buyer of the property on the quoted terms. You may be able to:

1 Rent out the property to a third party for two years for say, at least £500 per month, earning yourself £50 per month completely passive income.

And,

2 you may arrange to sell the same property in two years time at an agreed price of £57,500. Again, the buyer would still be getting a discount to market value but you would also be getting £2,500 (i.e. £57,500 less £55,000) for being in the middle.

Now clearly these figures are simple and of quite small value, but say you did 10 of these? or more? or the margins were bigger?

You could build an entire property portfolio income stream using this system where you did nothing but find the two parties (one seller and one buyer) and then sit there and collect the money – both income on a monthly basis and a lump sum at each option maturity. You would never own the properties at all!

In this case you could trade the lease options just like options in other commodities.

CONCLUSIONS

This section has been a run through of the new and perhaps creative ways of approaching property financing. The objective is writing this was to explain how all these things work so you as a potential property investor do not feel deterred by the mechanics of how these things are put together. Hopefully this has given you enough information – and confidence – to look at these schemes with a more informed mind.

There will have been sessions here that have caught your imagination and your enthusiasm for finding out more. So consider starting with that topic when you devise your own personal property investment strategy.

Whatever you decide to do, it is important that you use this information to take action and do something because we know that:

"It's not what you know but how you use it that counts!"

Final Top Tips

Finally, many people ask about the top financial tips for property investing, so here are some vital points to remember:

1   When looking at rental properties set yourself a minimum income amount – try £100 per property per month – and then don't accept any property that falls below this.

2   When considering interest rates set a limit of twice the base rate as the maximum you are prepared to pay for funding costs.

3   Losses on profits can be great as they are useful to offset against other profits – both income and gains – for tax purposes.

4   The key to getting a good financial deal is in the sourcing: if you can source 100 properties of the same type for your portfolio, you have strength when negotiating the purchase price, as there will also be somebody out of 100 owners who will accept a low price, which fits your strategy. If you only source 1 property, then the current owner has all the negotiating power.

5   Set your guide lines in terms of returns of cash inflows, percentage returns and capital requirements – and then just STICK to them! It makes the investing simple and emotionless if you have a procedure or system of returns and evaluation that you stick to.

6   Never borrow to spend only borrow to invest!

7   For every person who wishes to invest, there is a different strategy. No two people are alike so no two strategies will ever be the same.

8   The more you practice, the luckier you'll get.

9   Just ASK!

10   Have fun, and be grateful!

Gill Fielding

NOTES